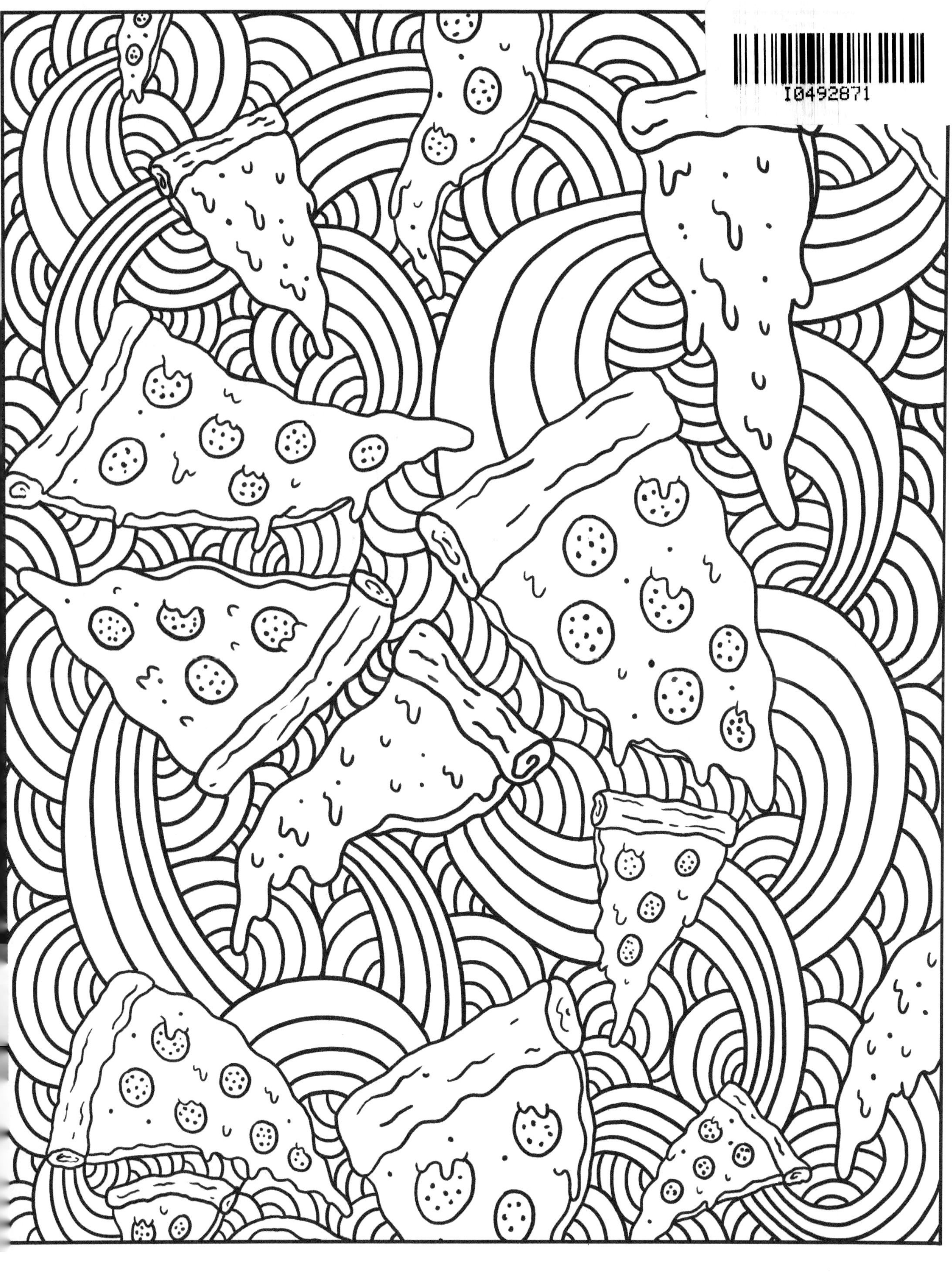

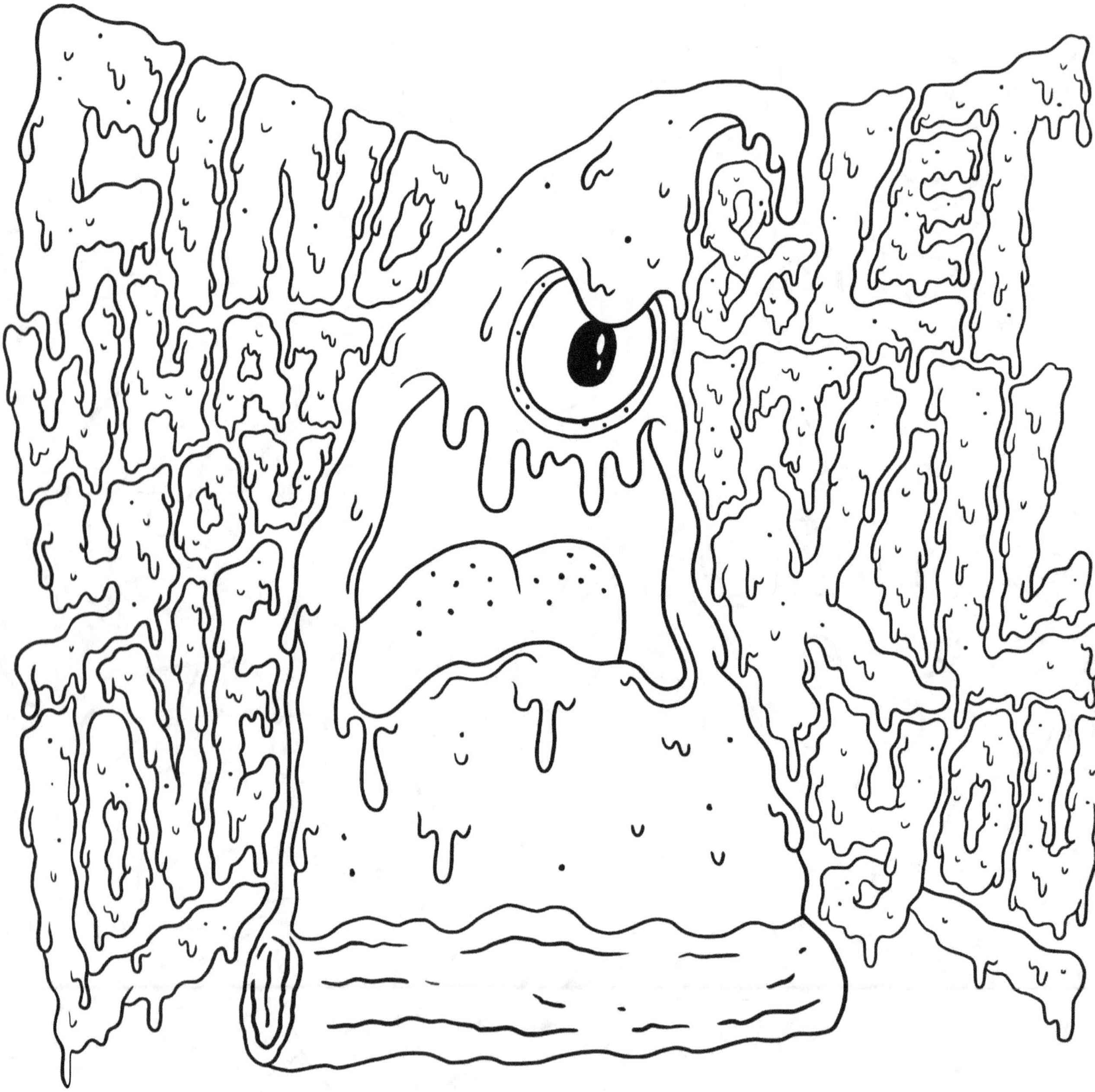
FIND WHAT YOU LOVE
& LET IT KILL YOU

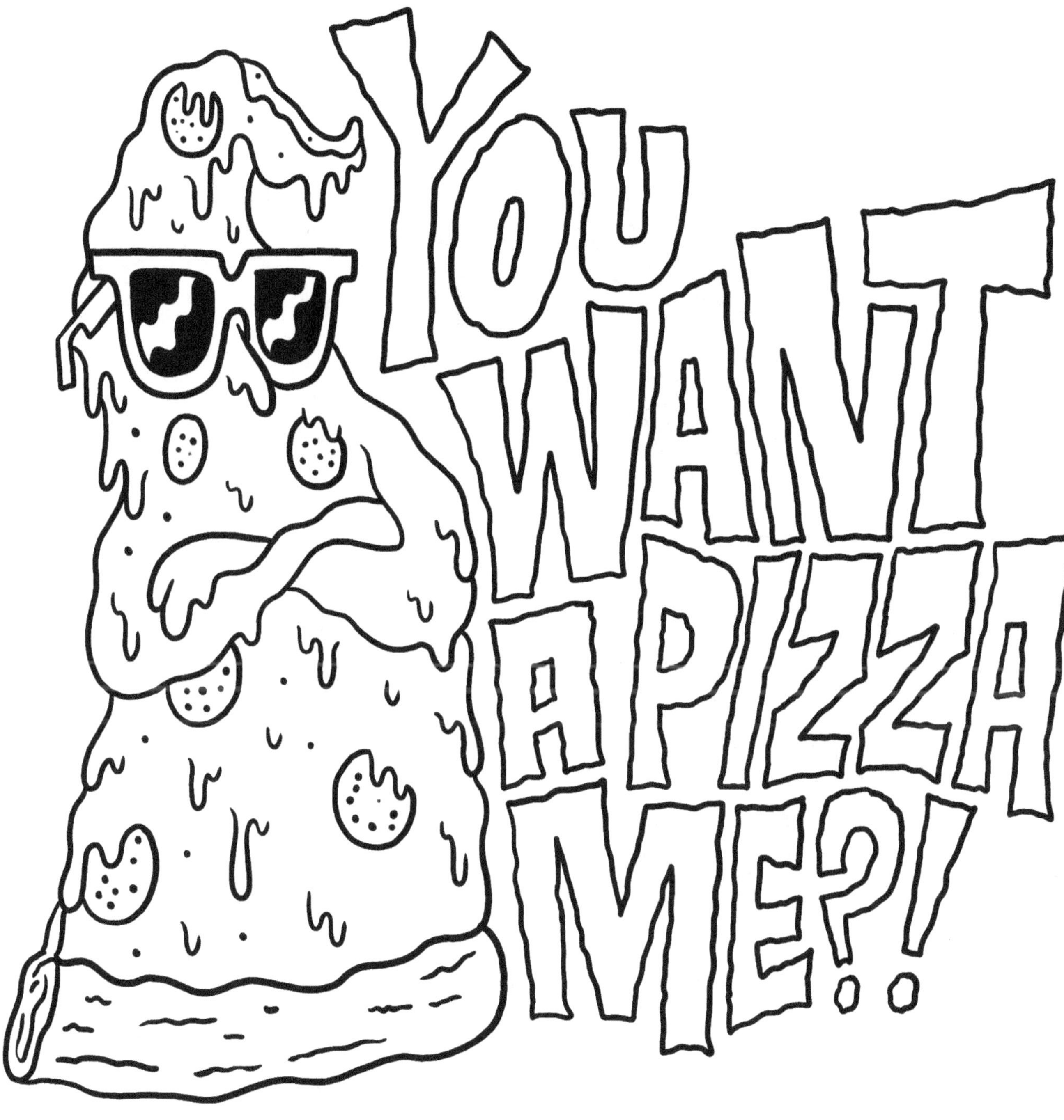
YOU
WANT
A PIZZA
ME?!

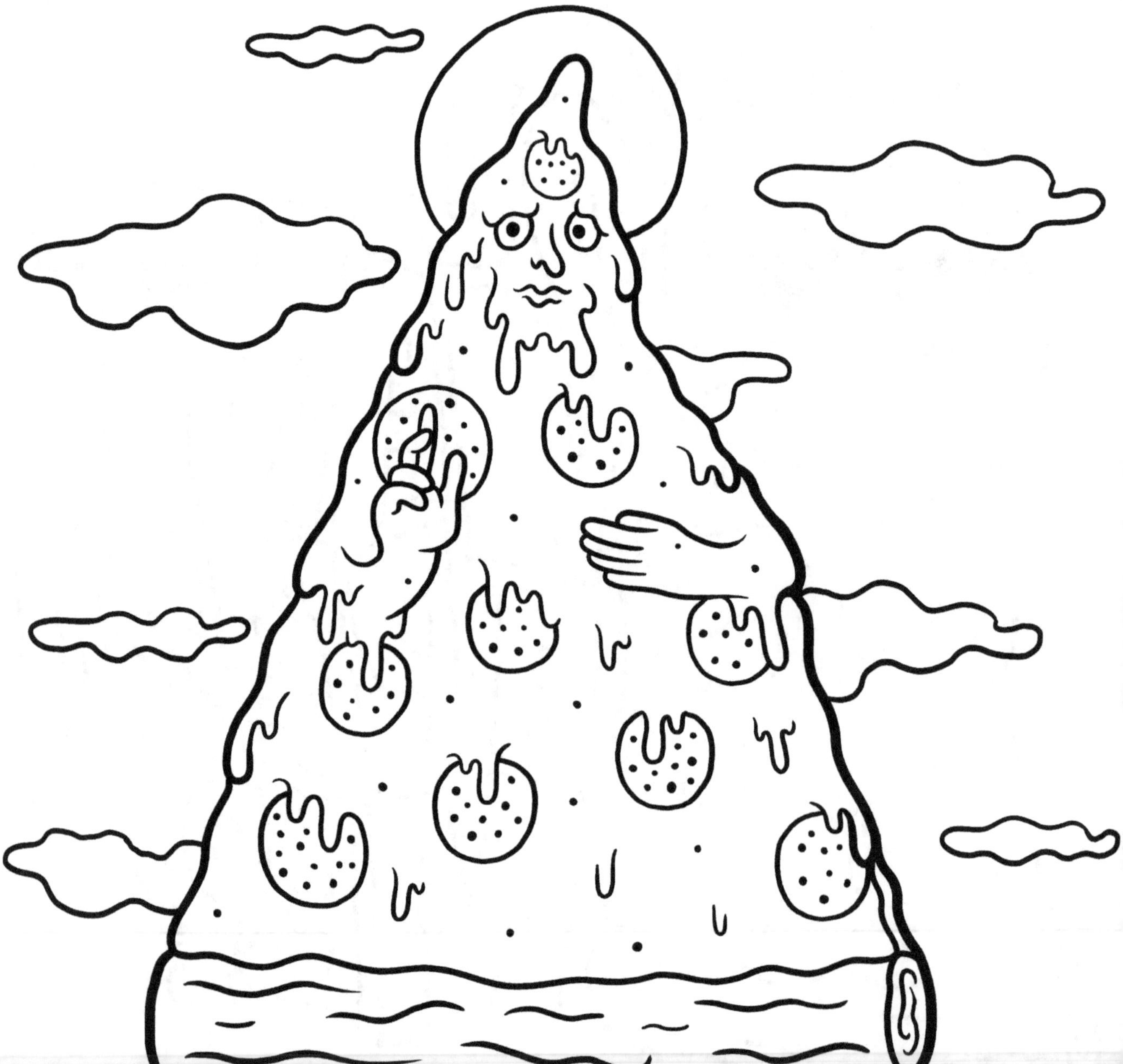

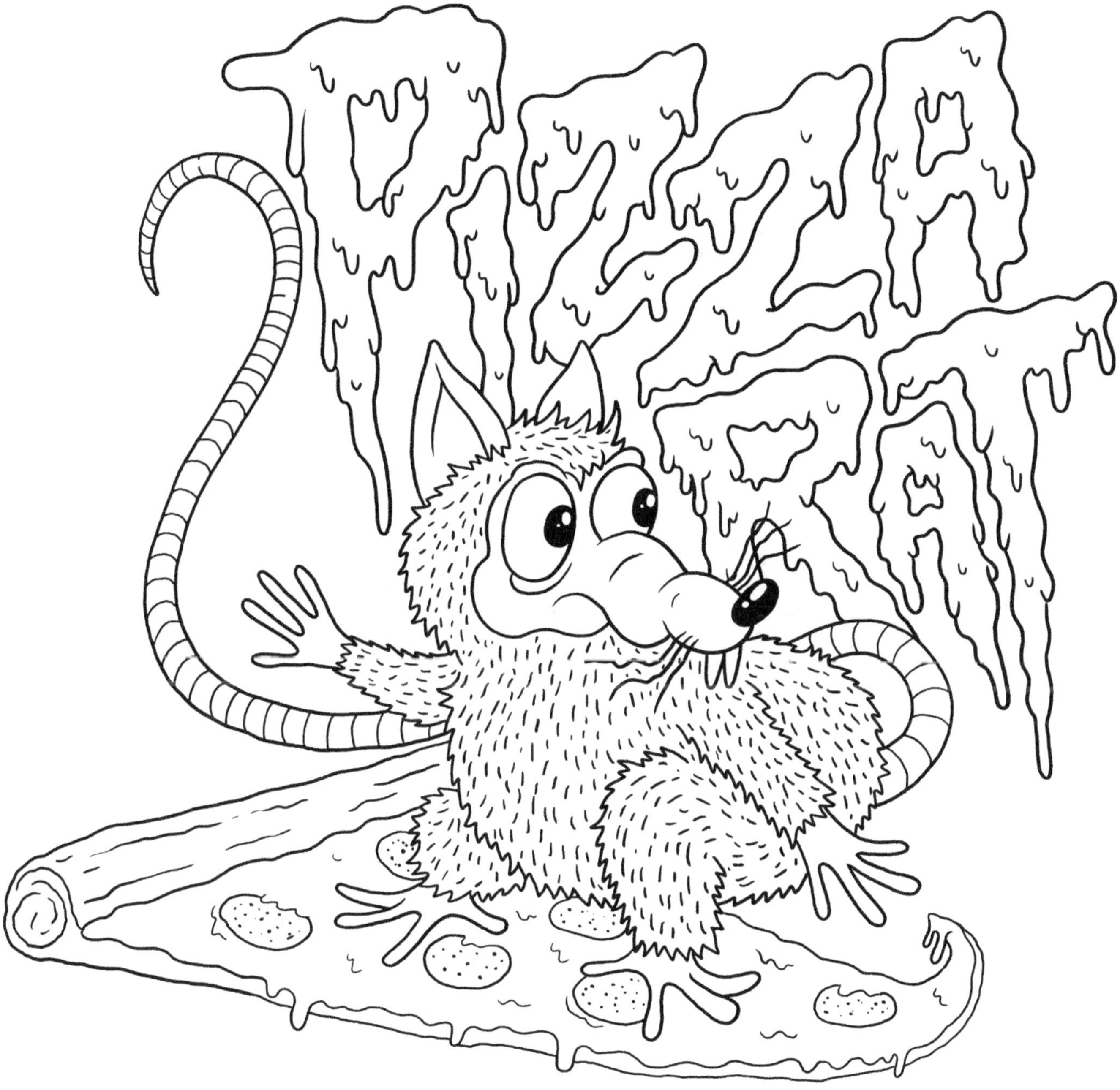
PIZZA RAT

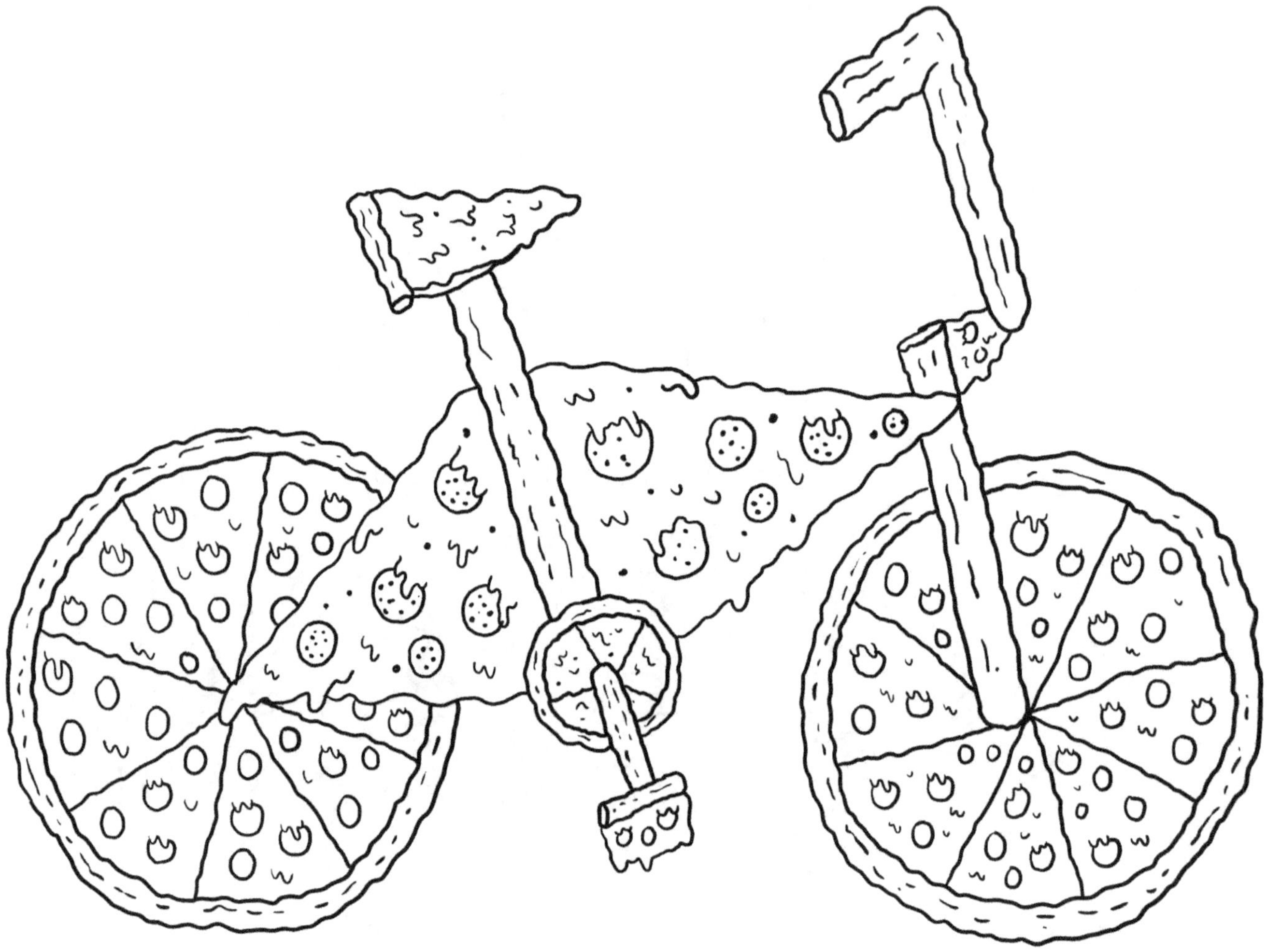

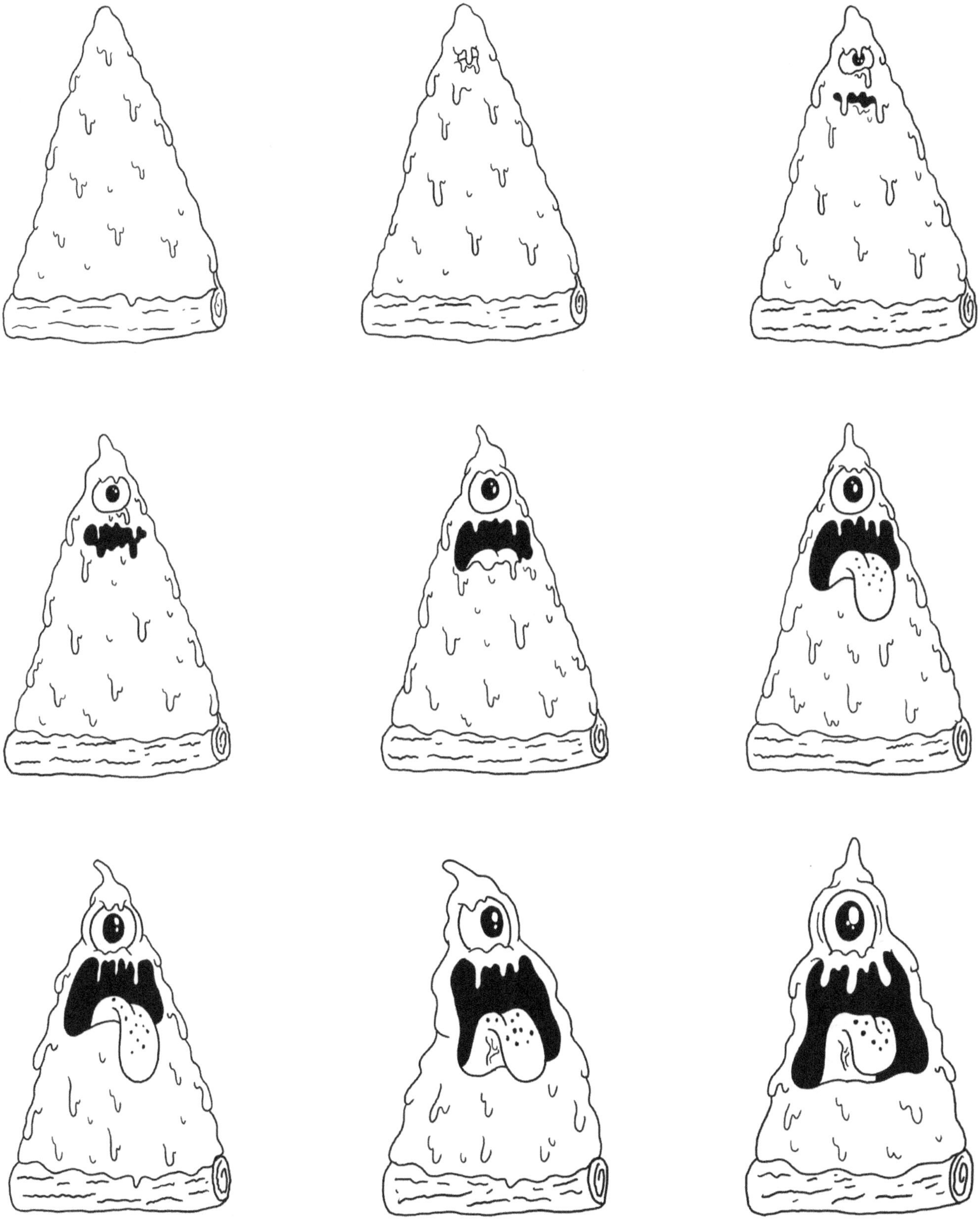

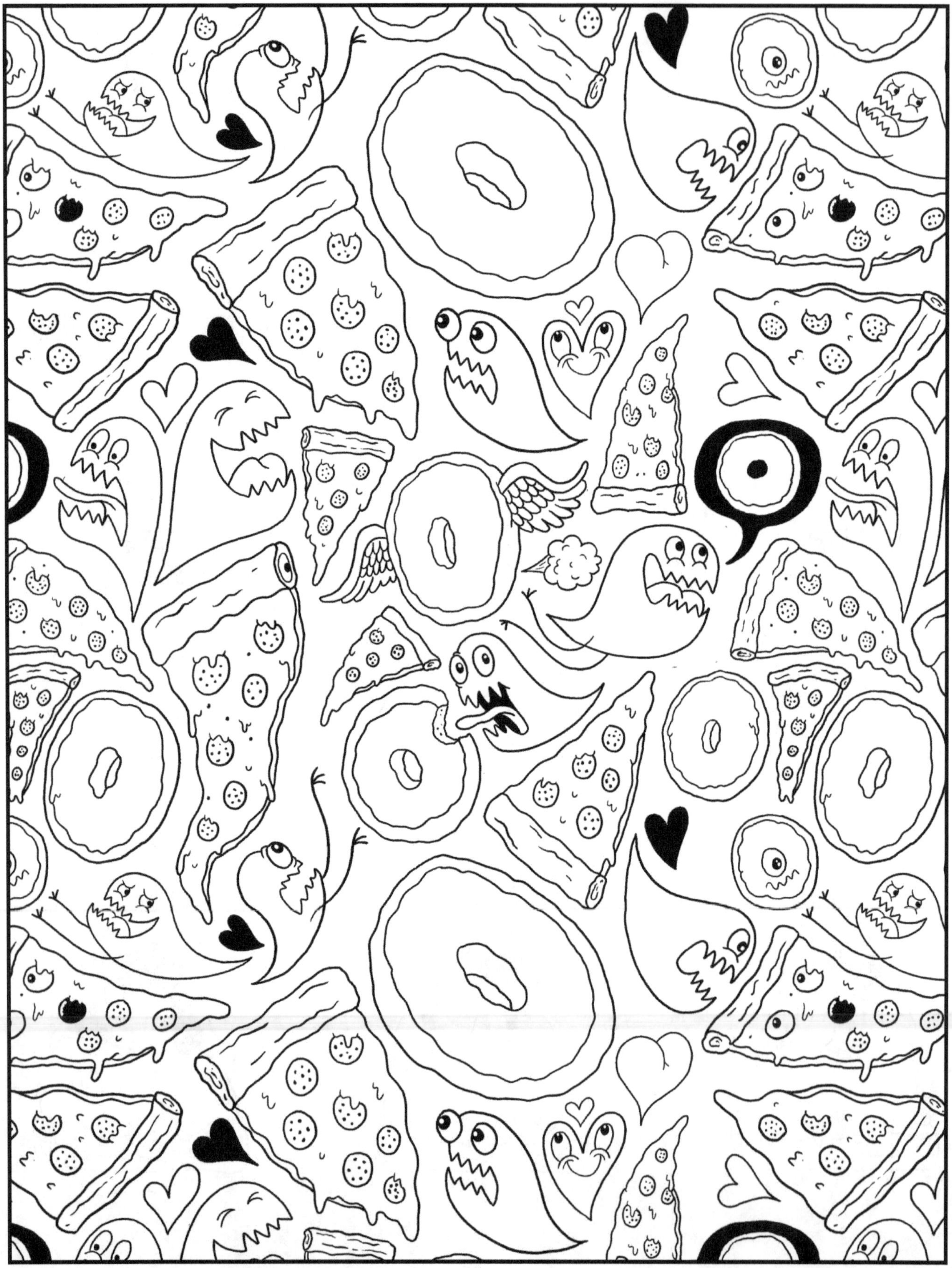

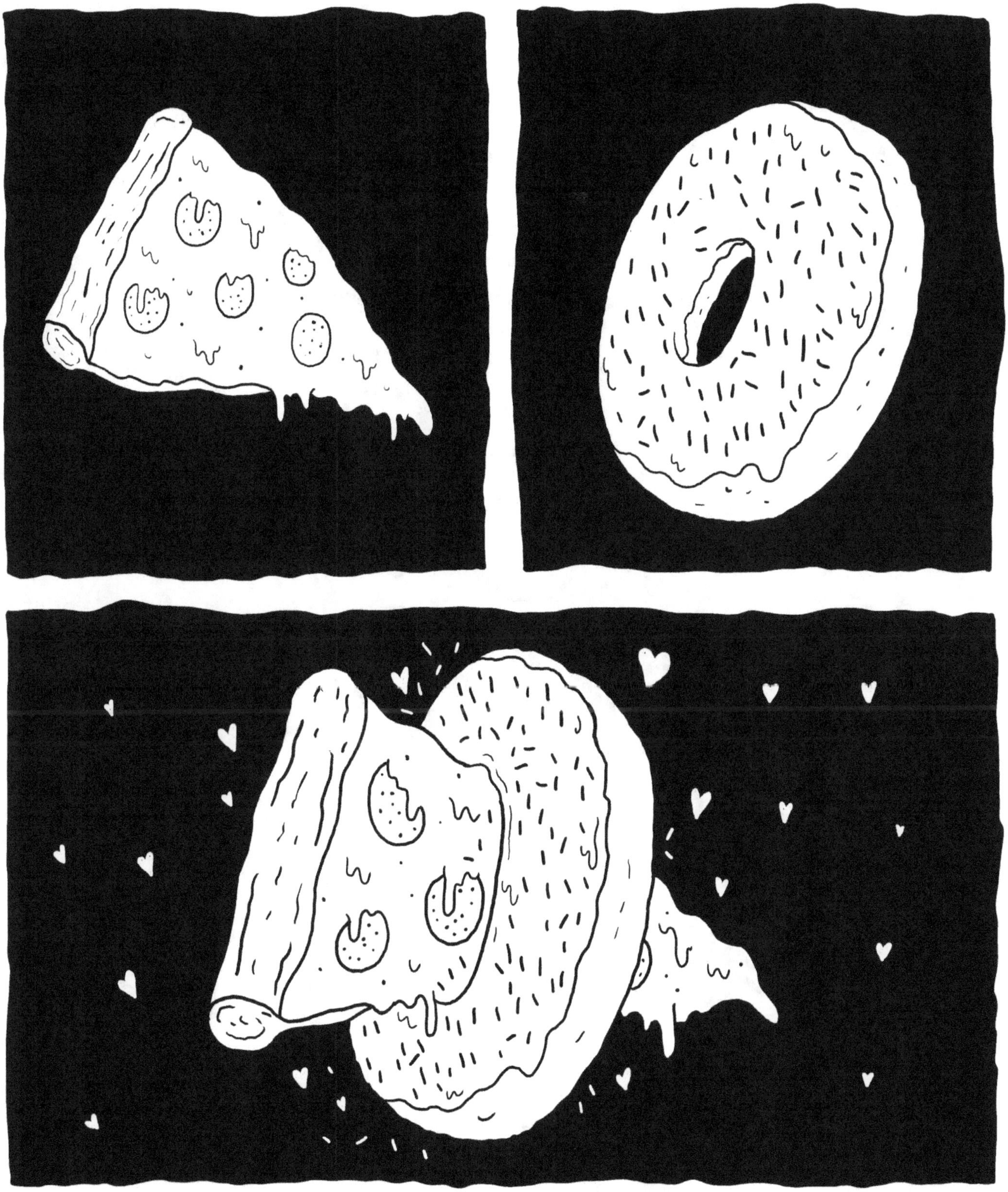

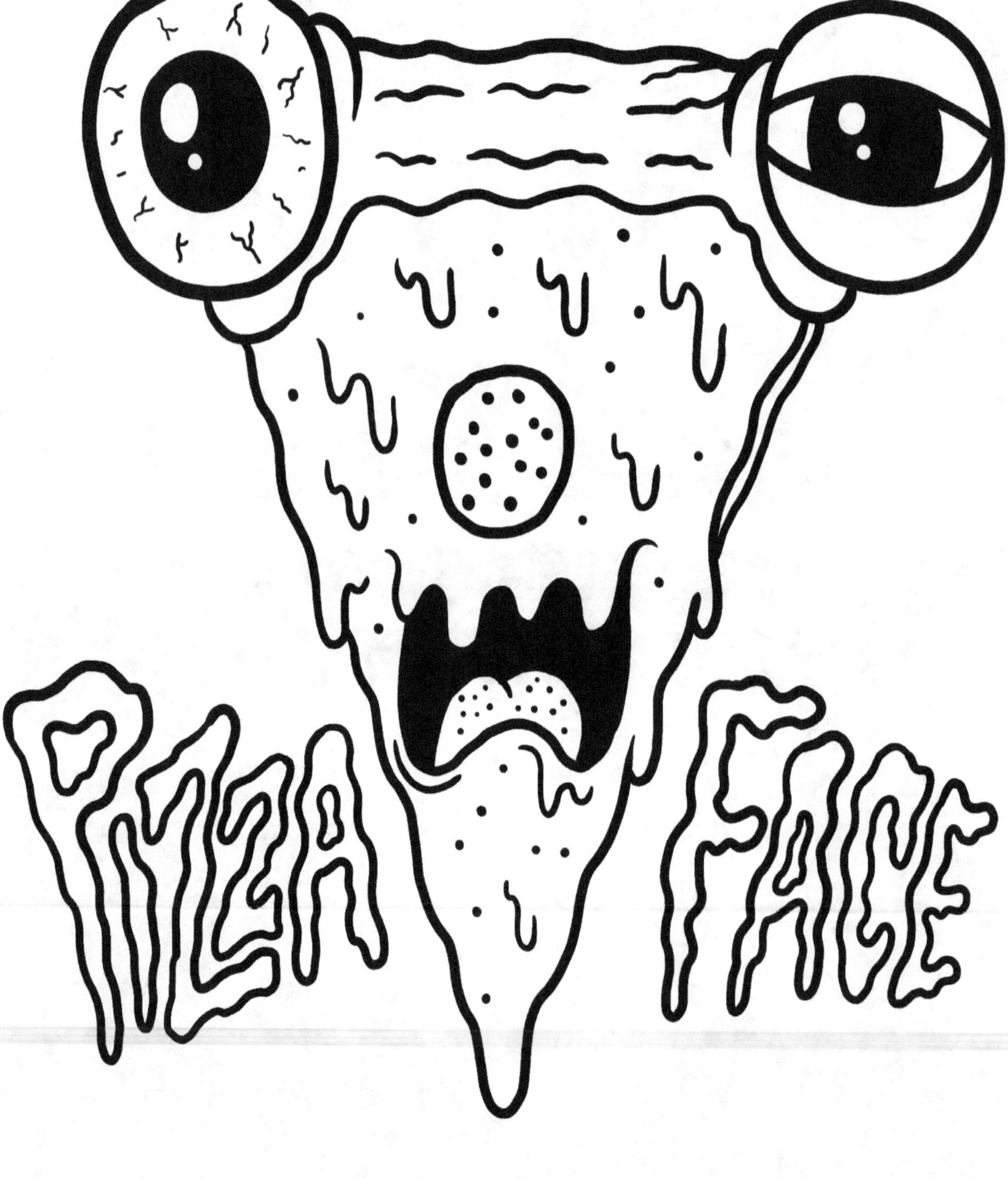
PIZZA FACE

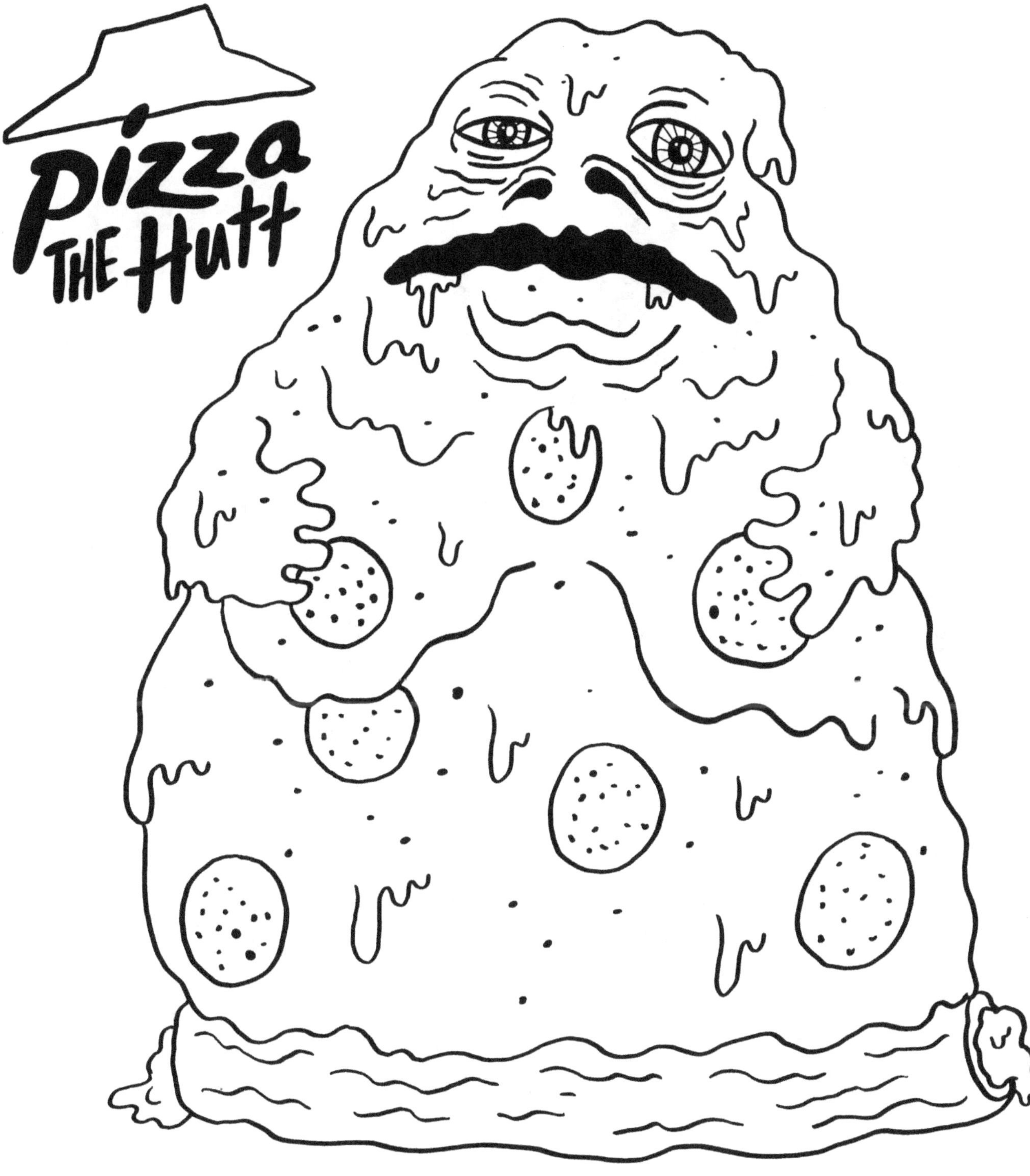
Pizza
THE Hutt

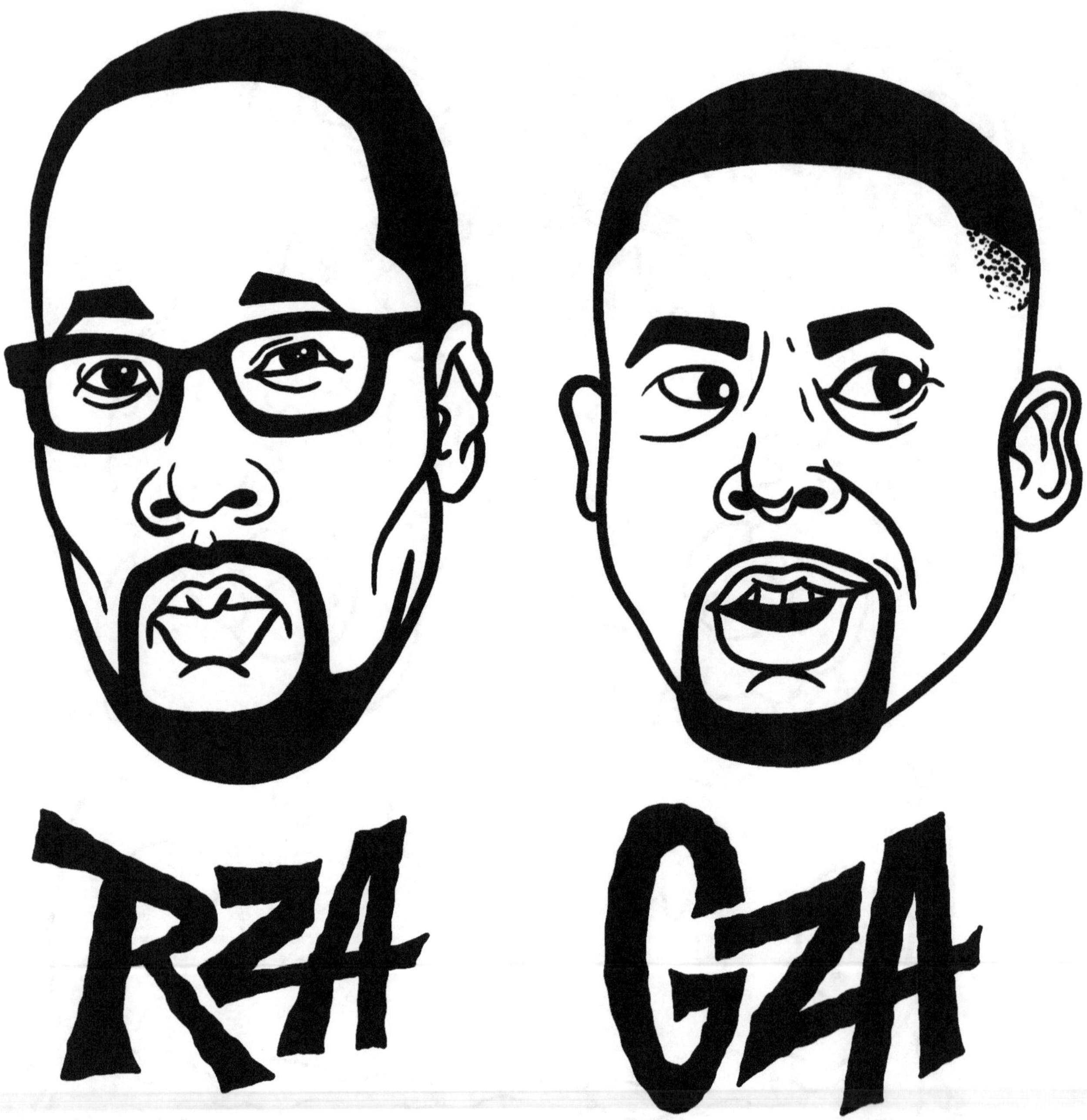
RZA
GZA

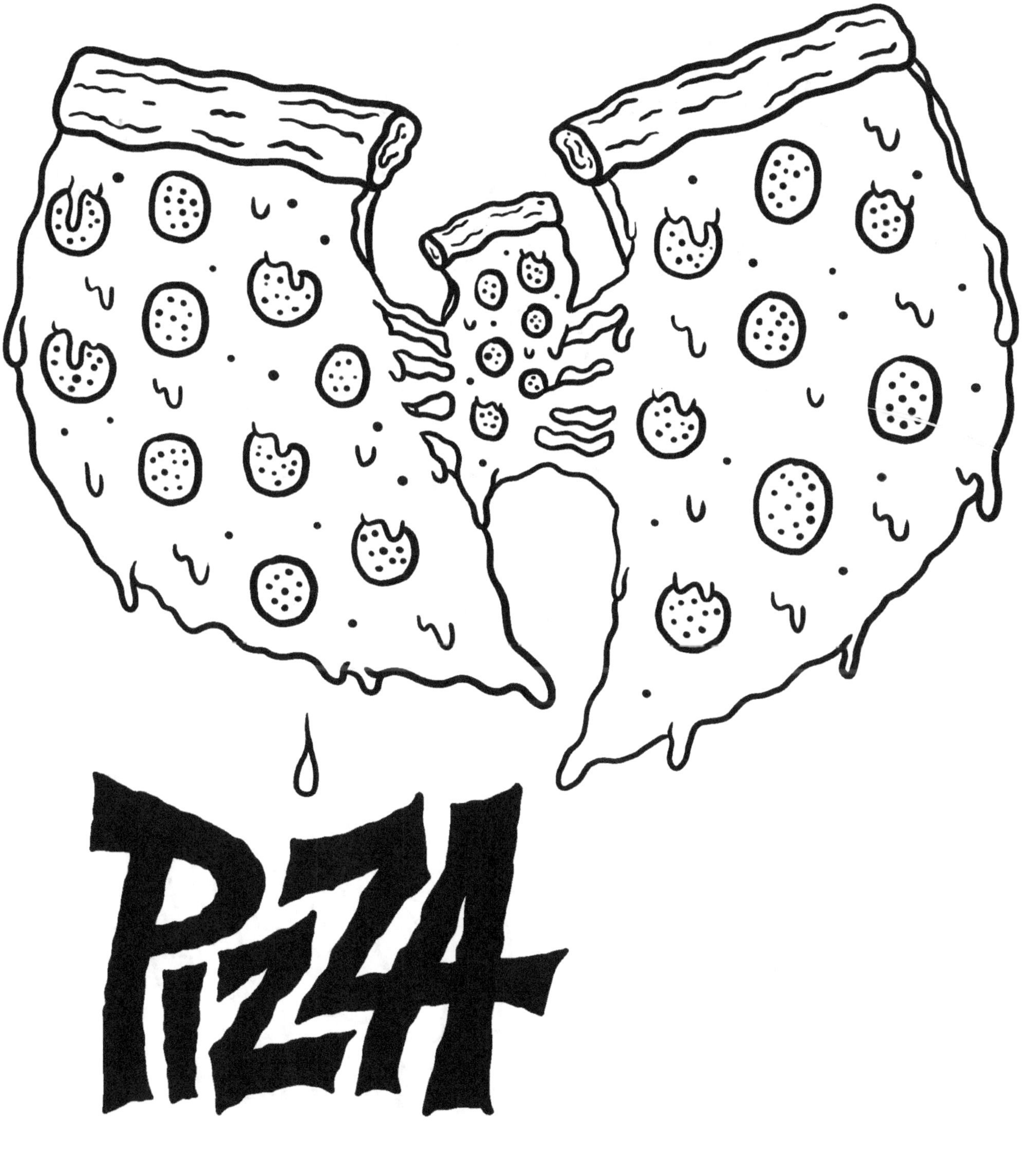
PIZZA

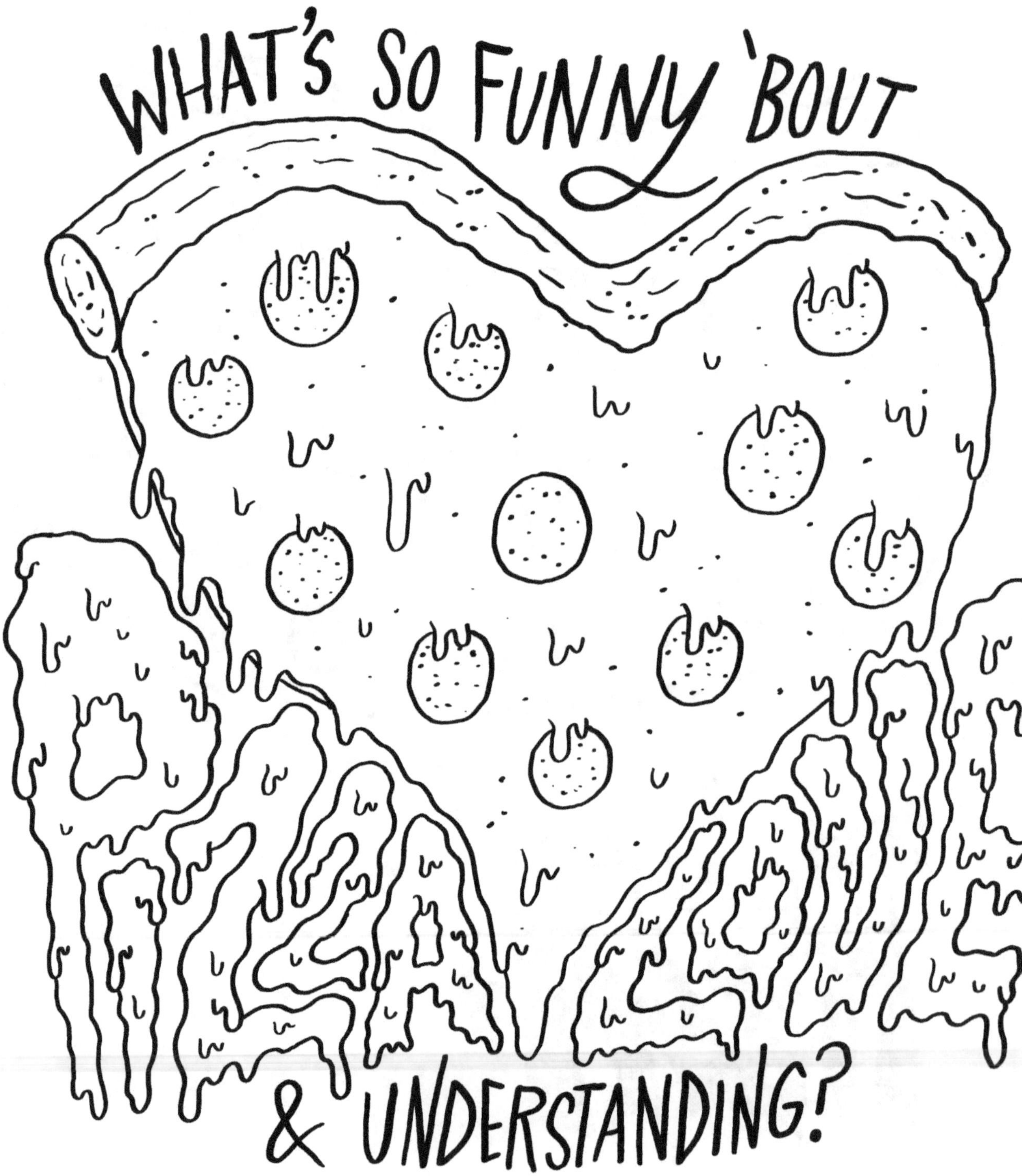
WHAT'S SO FUNNY 'BOUT
& UNDERSTANDING?

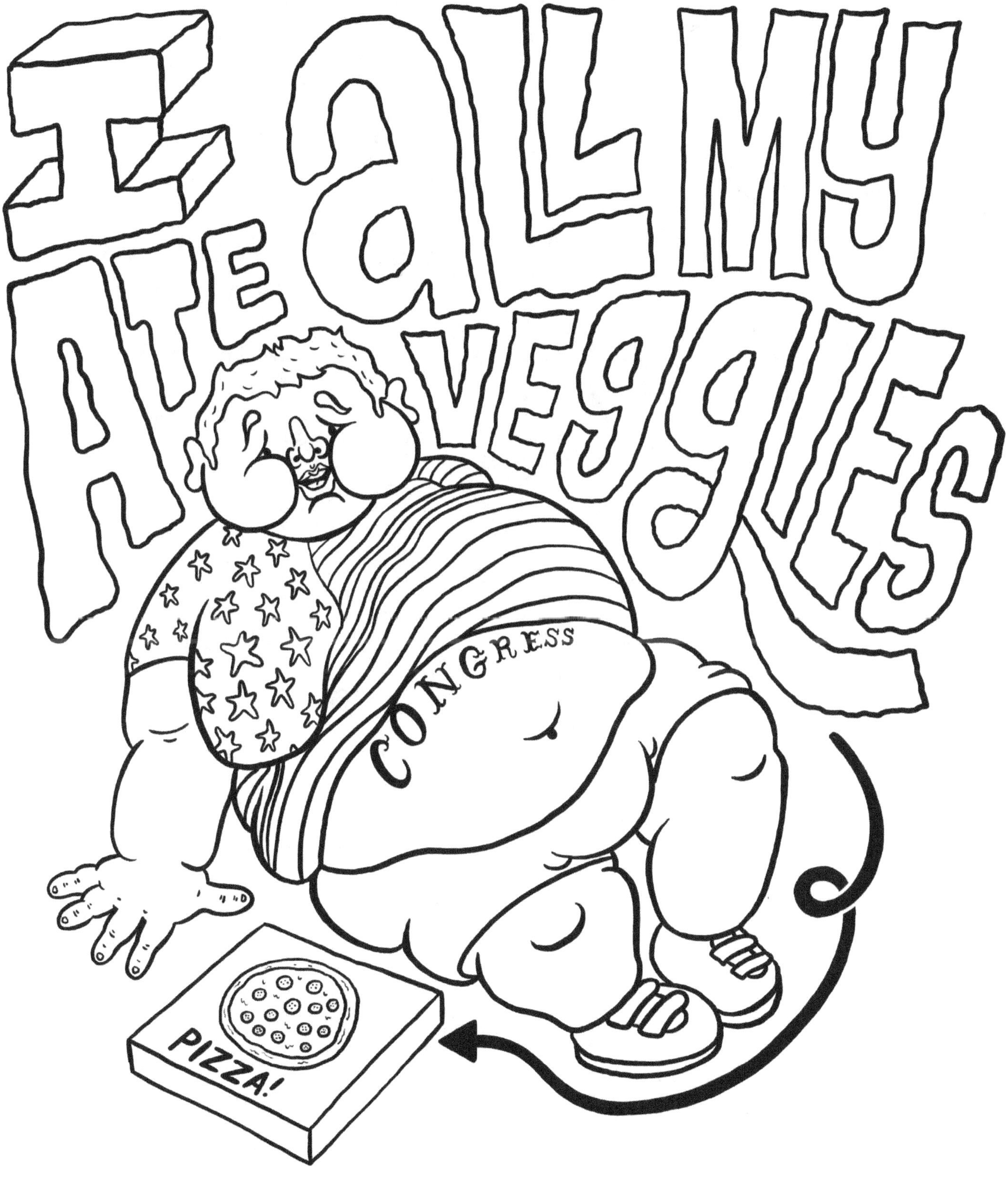

I ATE ALL MY VEGGIES
CONGRESS
PIZZA!

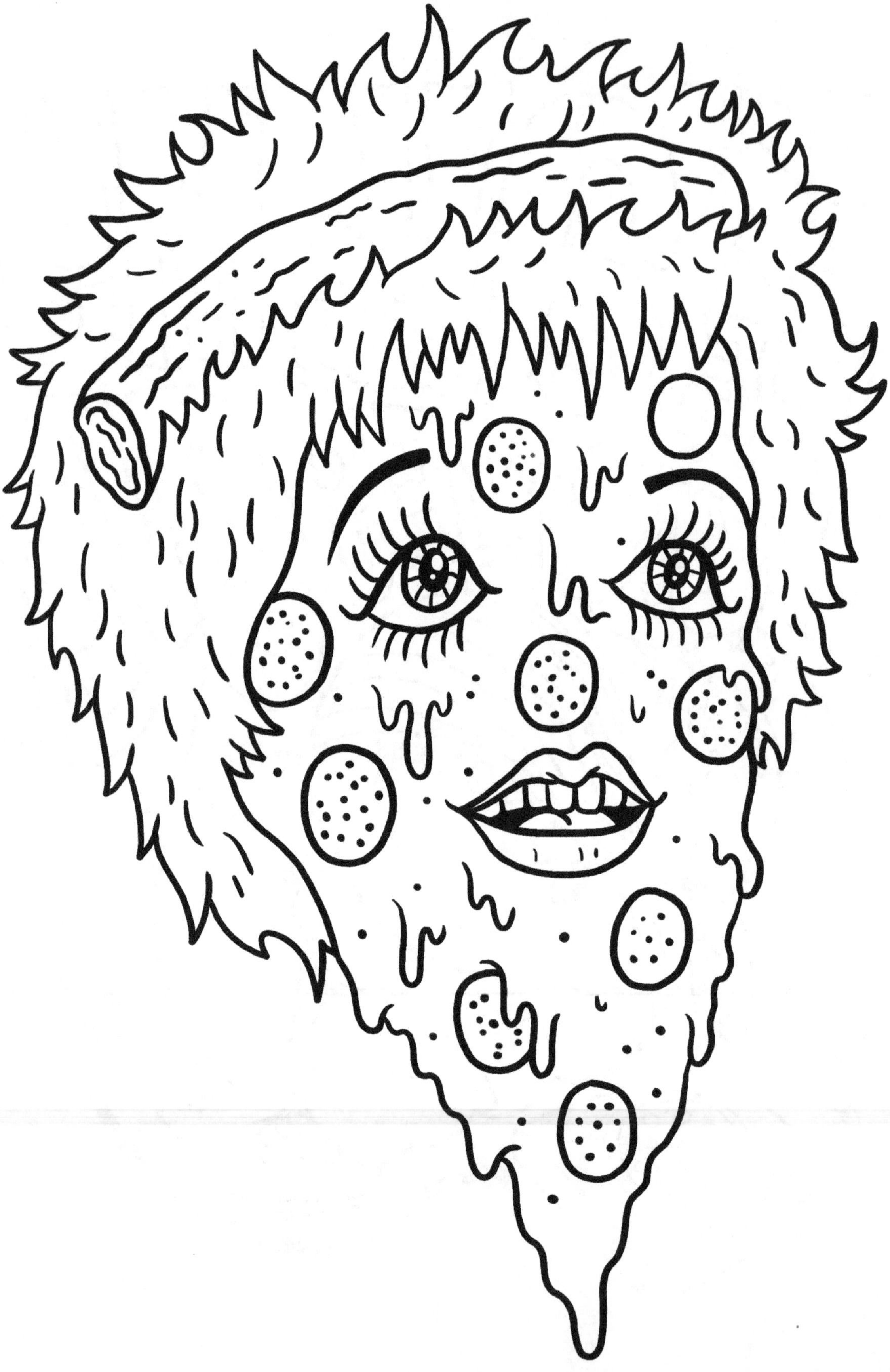

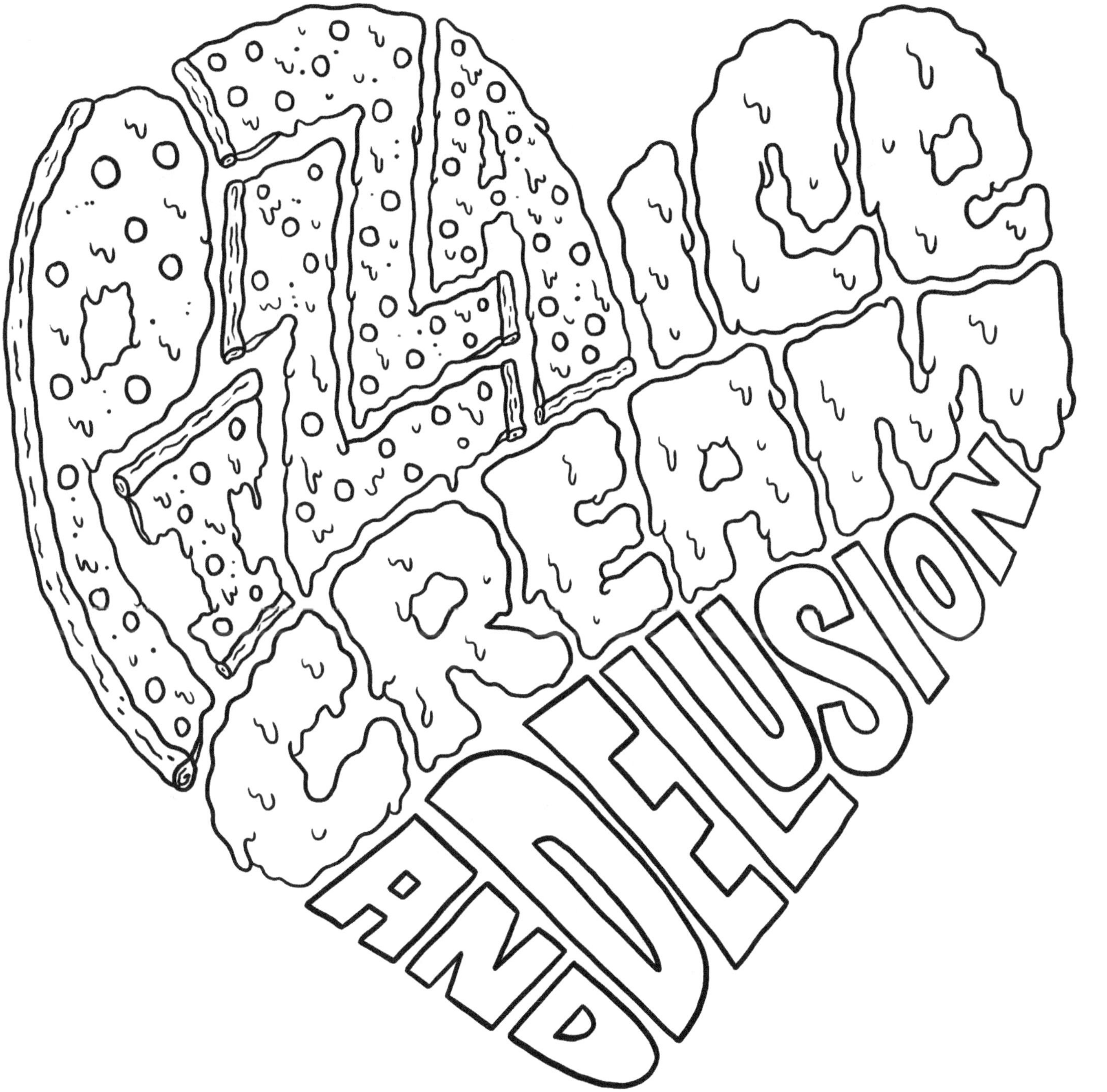
PIZZA
ICE CREAM
AND DELUSION

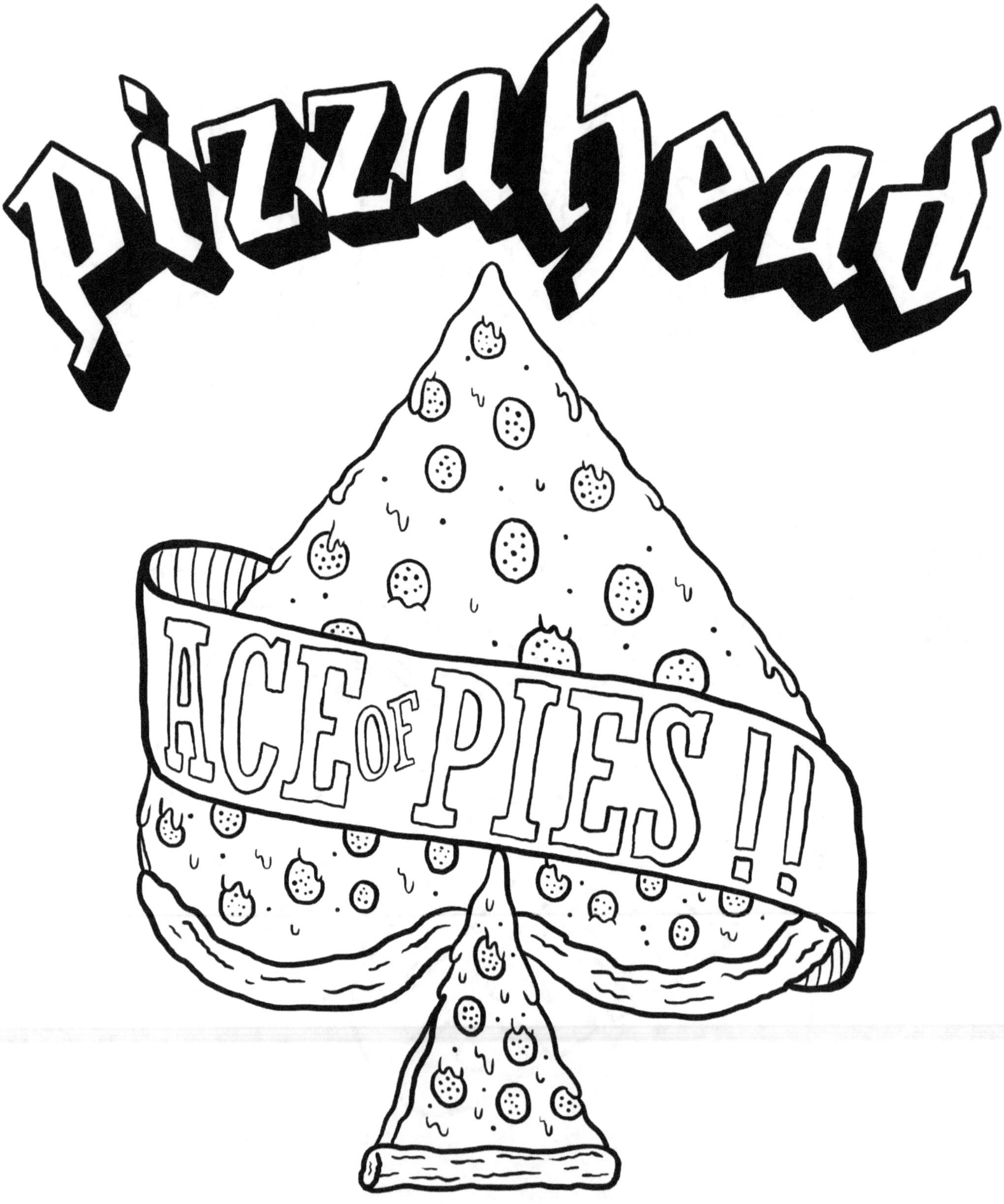
pizzahead
ACE OF PIES !!

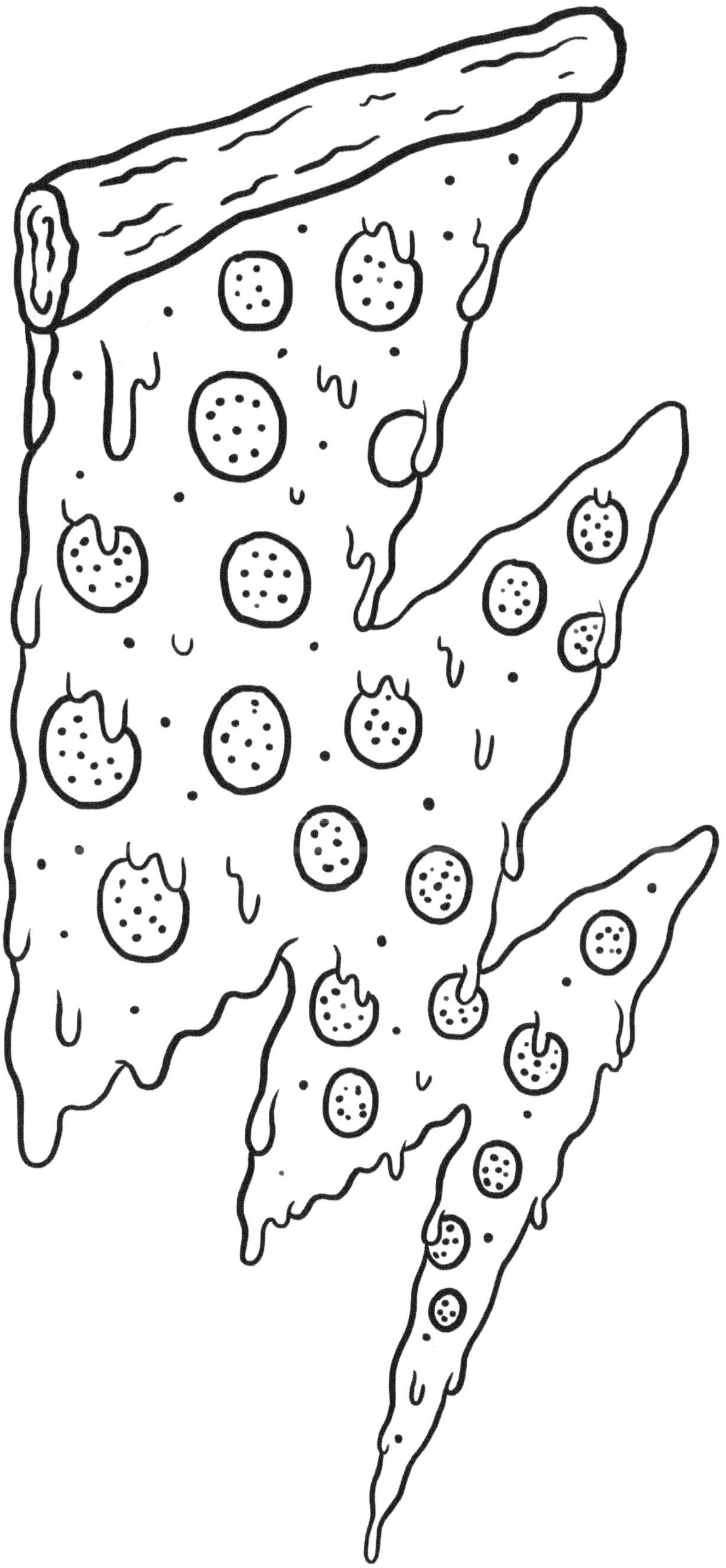

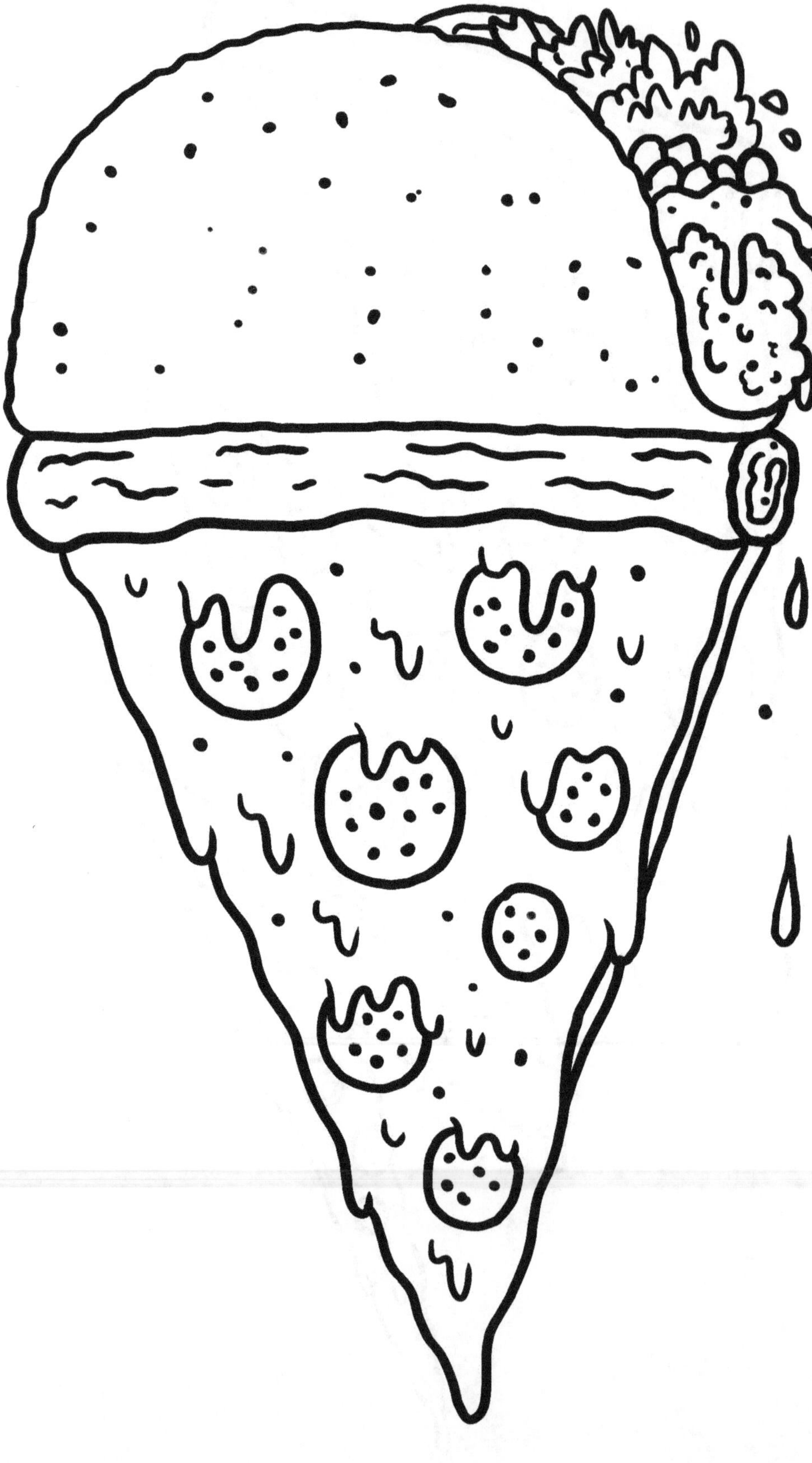

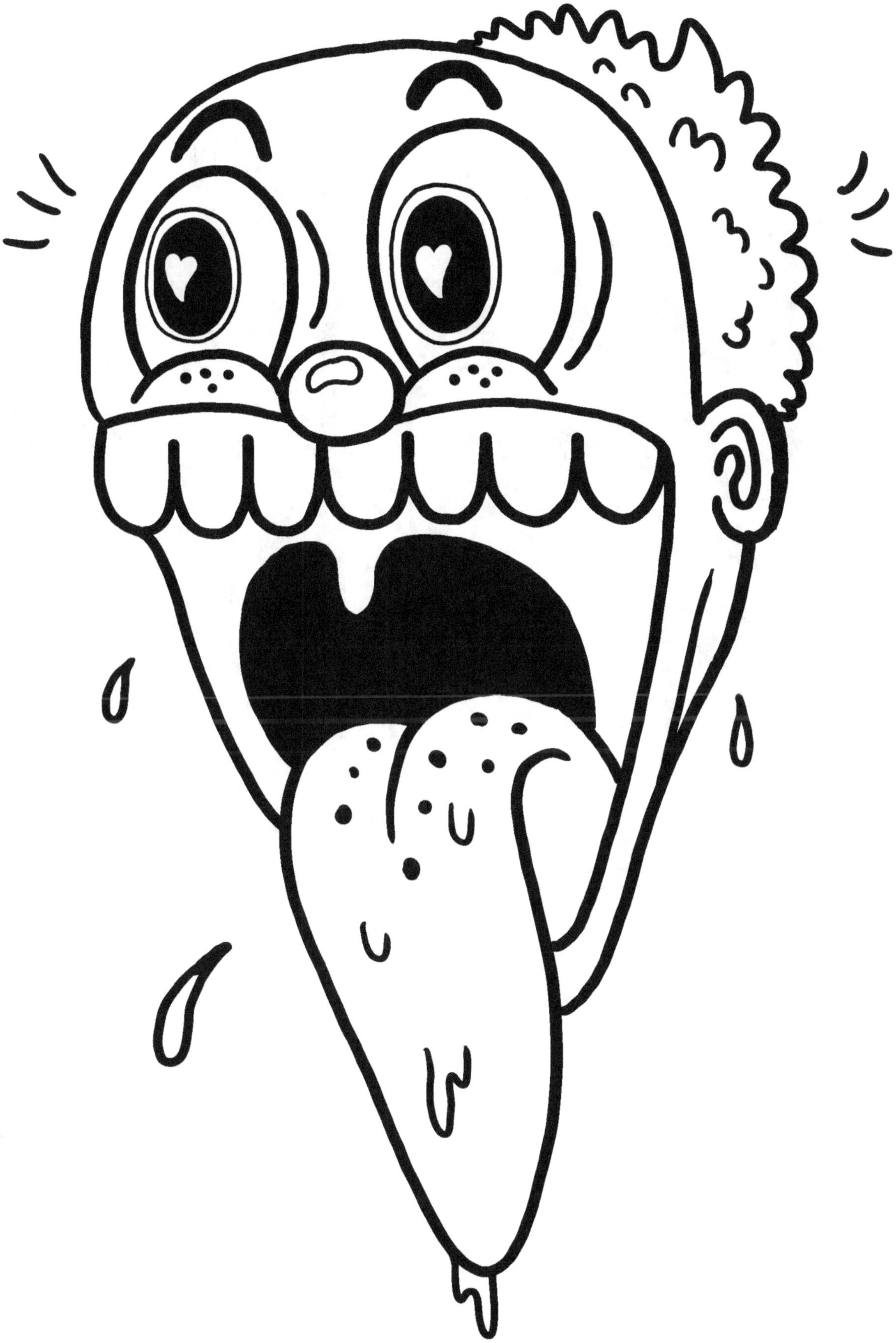

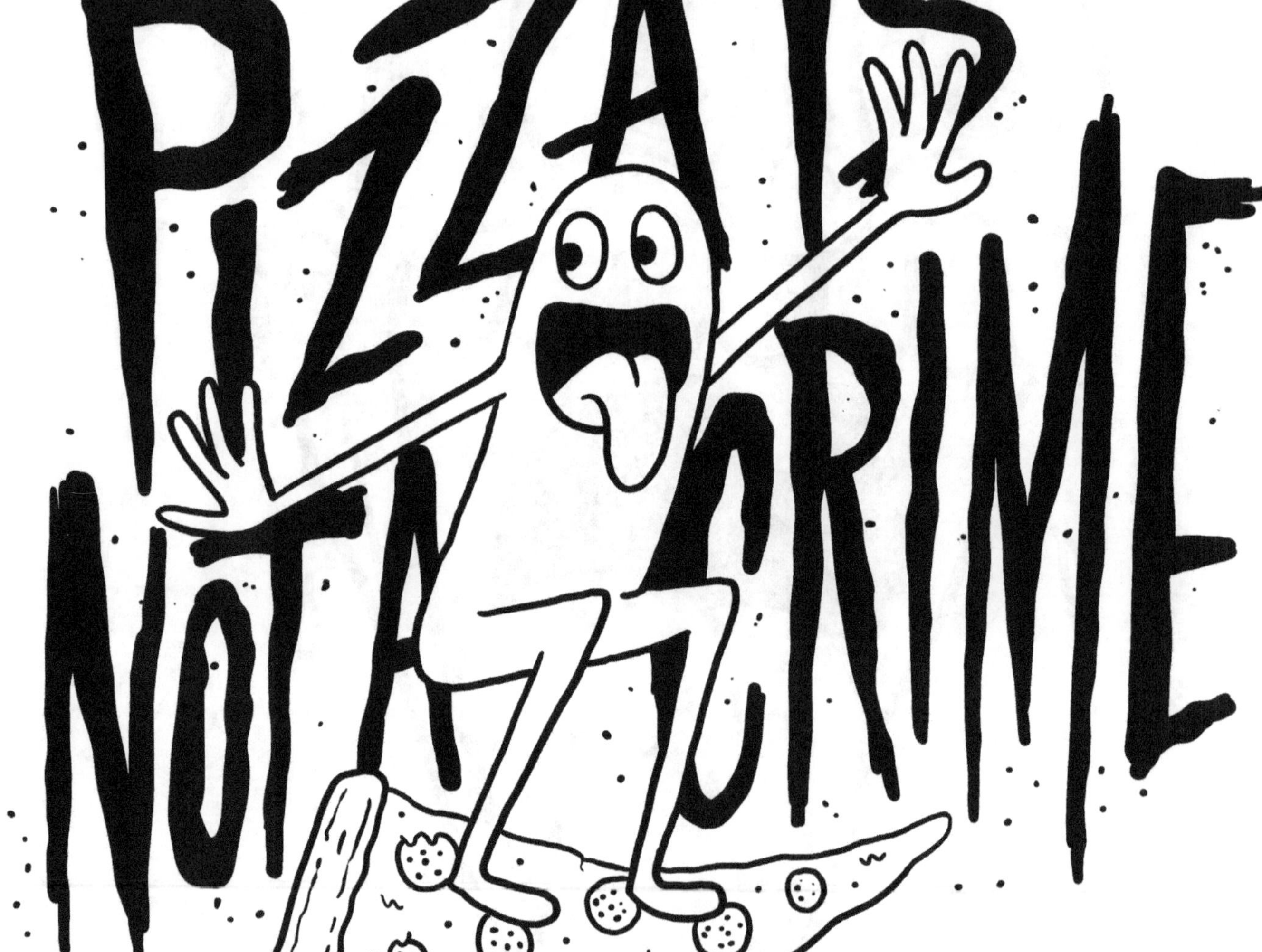
PIZZA IS
NOT A CRIME

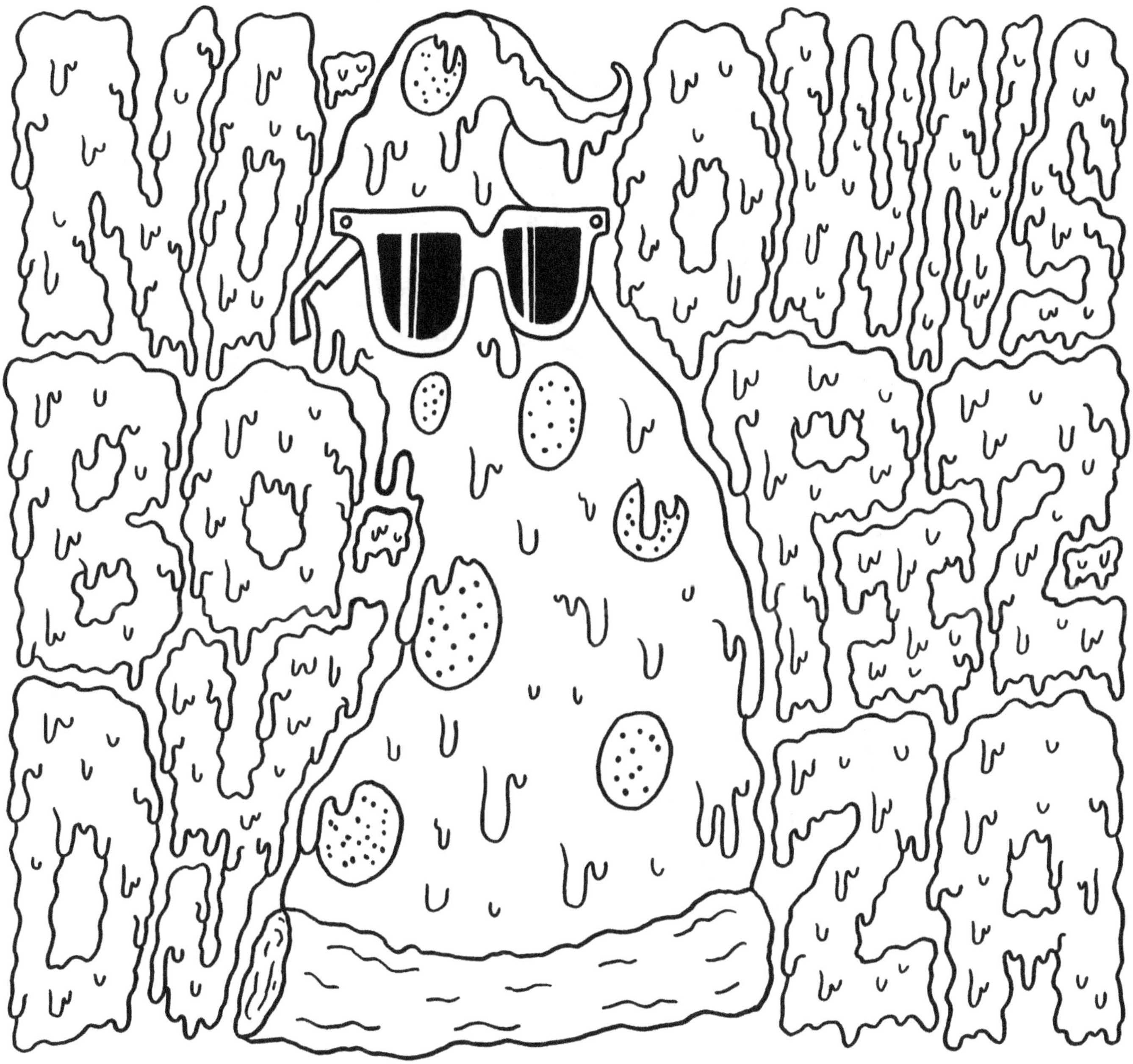
NO
BO
DY
OWNS
PIZ
ZA

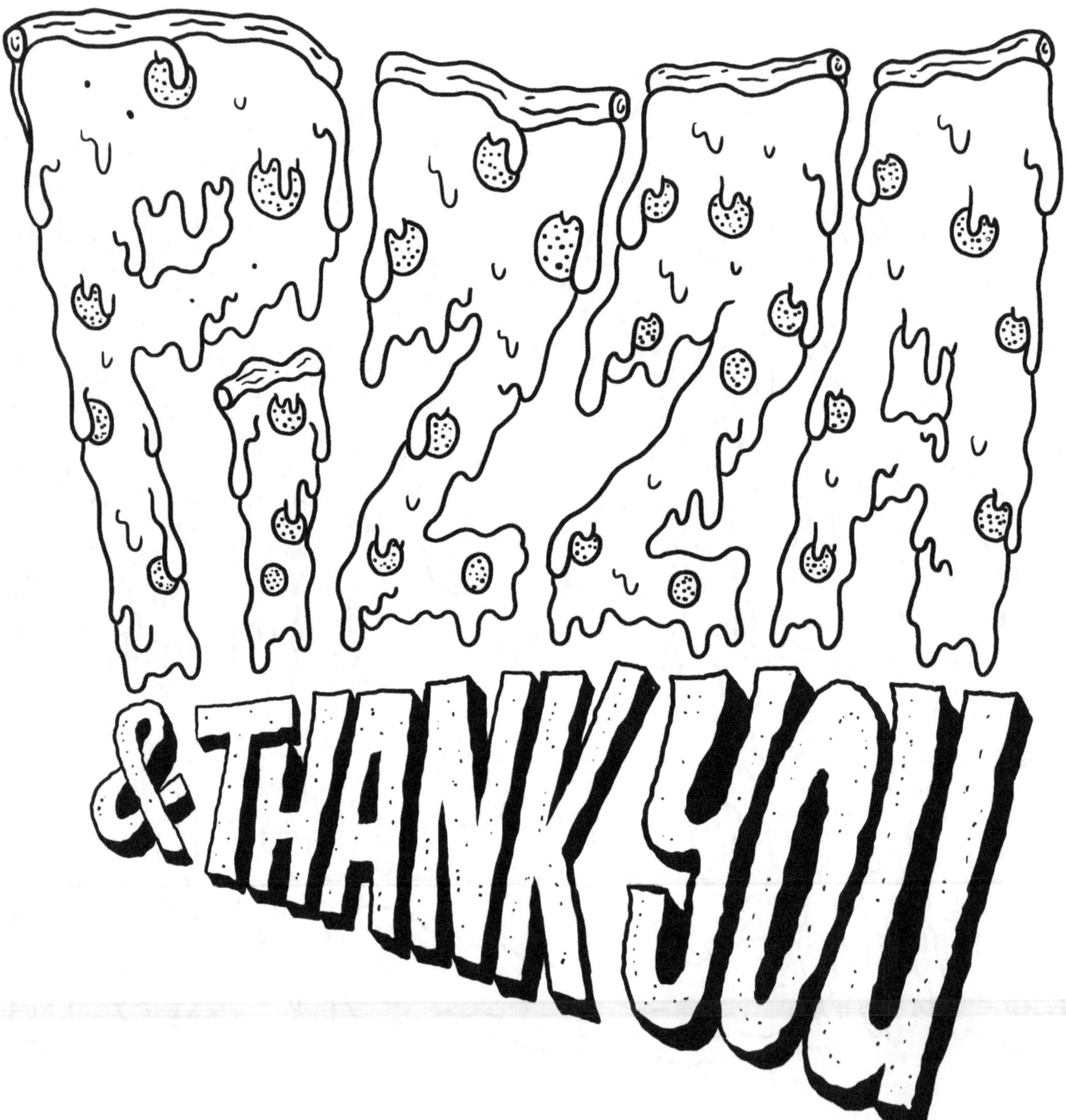
PIZZA
& THANK YOU

www.ingramcontent.com/pod-product-compliance
Lightning Source LLC
Chambersburg PA
CBHW080646190526
45169CB00009B/3520